Introduction to Marriage Laws in India

By Siva Prasad Bose

Published by Joy Bose

Copyright 2022 Siva Prasad Bose

All Rights Reserved

Dedication

This book is dedicated to all the people in India who are thinking of getting married or have got married and can benefit from the knowledge of existing marriage laws.

Contents

Dedication

Preface

Chapter 1: What is a Valid Marriage

Chapter 2: What Makes a Marriage Invalid

Chapter 3: What are the Grounds for Divorce

Chapter 4: Aspects of Divorce and Separation

Chapter 5: Schizophrenia and Mental Disorders as a Ground for Divorce

Chapter 6: Mental Cruelty as a Ground for Divorce

Chapter 7: Domicile for matrimonial cases and division of property

Chapter 8: 498a and Domestic Violence Act

Chapter 9: Conclusion

Appendix A: The Hindu Marriage Act 1955

Glossary of Legal Terms

Acknowledgments

About the author

Other Books by Siva Prasad Bose

Preface

Marriage laws form a vital part of India's legal system, particularly in cases where marital relationships face challenges such as disputes, separation, or breakdown. These laws are essential not only for resolving conflicts but also for protecting the rights and responsibilities of individuals in a marriage.

This book is designed to serve as a practical guide to understanding the complexities of marriage laws in India. Written in a simple and accessible style, it provides readers with a clear overview of what constitutes a valid or invalid marriage, the legal processes for divorce and separation, and the rights of spouses under Indian law. Topics such as annulment, mental cruelty, property rights, and legal safeguards like Section 498a and the Domestic Violence Act are discussed in detail.

By exploring both the legal and practical aspects of marriage laws, this book aims to empower individuals with knowledge that can help them navigate marital challenges more effectively. Whether you are preparing for marriage, facing a marital dispute, or simply seeking to expand your understanding of the legal framework, this book is a valuable resource.

It is our hope that this work will not only inform but also inspire readers to approach marriage with greater awareness of their rights and obligations, fostering relationships that are not only lawful but also harmonious and respectful.

Chapter 1: What is a Valid Marriage

Marriage in India is both a social institution and a legal contract governed by specific laws. These laws ensure the validity of marriages, protect the rights of spouses, and provide mechanisms for resolving disputes. This chapter explores Indian marriage laws, offering insights into legal provisions and real-life applications.

We begin with an overview of marriage laws and their historical evolution, examining their relevance in contemporary Indian society. Subsequent sections delve into various acts governing different communities, such as the Hindu Marriage Act, the Special Marriage Act, and others, alongside discussions on annulment, divorce, and maintenance. By the end of this chapter, readers will have a comprehensive understanding of the legal requirements for a valid marriage.

1.1 Laws related to marriages in India: Hindu Marriage Act 1955

The Hindu Marriage Act, 1955 governs marriages among Hindus, including Buddhists, Jains, and Sikhs. It outlines the conditions for a valid marriage, such as:

- **Monogamy:** Both parties must not have a living spouse at the time of the marriage.

- **Mental Capacity:** Both parties must be capable of giving valid consent.

- **Prohibited Degrees of Relationship:** Parties must not fall within prohibited relationships unless permitted by custom.

- **Sapinda Relationship:** Parties must not share lineage within three generations on the paternal side or five generations on the maternal side unless allowed by custom.

Example of a Valid Marriage: Ravi and Priya, both Hindus, meet all the conditions outlined in the Act, including being of legal age and not related within prohibited degrees. Their marriage is legally valid.

Example of an Invalid Marriage: If Ravi and Priya were cousins within the prohibited degrees of relationship, their marriage would be invalid unless an exception under custom applied.

THE HINDU MARRIAGE ACT, 1955

ACT No. 25 OF 1955[1]

[18th May, 1955.]

An act to amend and codify the law relating to marriage among Hindus.

BE it enacted by Parliament in the Sixth Year of the Republic of India as follows:—

PRELIMINARY

1. Short title and extent.—(*1*) This Act may be called the Hindu Marriage Act, 1955.

(*2*) It extends to the whole of India except the State of Jammu and Kashmir, and applies also to Hindus domiciled in the territories to which this Act extends who are outside the said territories.

2. Application of Act.—(*1*) This Act applies—

(*a*) to any person who is a Hindu by religion in any of its forms or developments, including a Virashaiva, a Lingayat or a follower of the Brahmo, Prarthana or Arya Samaj,

(*b*) to any person who is a Buddhist, Jaina or Sikh by religion, and

(*c*) to any other person domiciled in the territories to which this Act extends who is not a Muslim, Christian, Parsi or Jew by religion, unless it is proved that any such person would not have been governed by the Hindu law or by any custom or usage as part of that law in respect of any of the matters dealt with herein if this Act had not been passed.

Explanation.—The following persons are Hindus, Buddhists, Jainas or Sikhs by religion, as the case may be:—

(*a*) any child, legitimate or illegitimate, both of whose parents are Hindus, Buddhists, Jainas or Sikhs by religion;

(*b*) any child, legitimate or illegitimate, one of whose parents is a Hindu, Buddhist, Jaina or Sikh by religion and who is brought up as a member of the tribe, community, group or family to which such parent belongs or belonged; and

(*c*) any person who is a convert or re-convert to the Hindu, Buddhist, Jaina or Sikh religion.

(*2*) Notwithstanding anything contained in sub-section (*1*), nothing contained in this Act shall apply to the members of any Scheduled tribe within the meaning of clause (*25*) of article 366 of the Constitution unless the Central Government, by notification in the Official Gazette, otherwise directs.

(*3*) The expression "Hindu" in any portion of this Act shall be construed as if it included a person who, though not a Hindu by religion, is, nevertheless, a person to whom this Act applies by virtue of the provisions contained in this section.

Figure: Opening of the Hindu Marriage Act 1955

1.2 Conditions for a valid marriage as per the Hindu Marriage Act

The Hindu Marriage Act specifies the following conditions for a valid marriage:

- **Ceremonial Requirements (Section 7)**: The marriage must be solemnized in accordance with the customary rites and ceremonies of either party. If the ceremony includes Saptapadi (seven steps before the sacred fire), this requirement must be fulfilled.

- **No Existing Marriage (Section 5(i))**: Neither party should have a subsisting valid marriage with any other person.

- **Legal Age and Mental Capacity (Sections 5(ii) and (iii))**: Both parties must meet the minimum legal age requirement (21 for males and 18 for females) and have the mental capacity to understand the nature of marriage.

- **Prohibited Degrees and Sapinda Relationship (Section 5(iv))**: Parties must not be within prohibited degrees of relationship or a sapinda relationship unless permitted by custom.

Figure: Photo of the Saptapadi marriage ritual in Hindu marriages: taking seven steps around the sacred fire

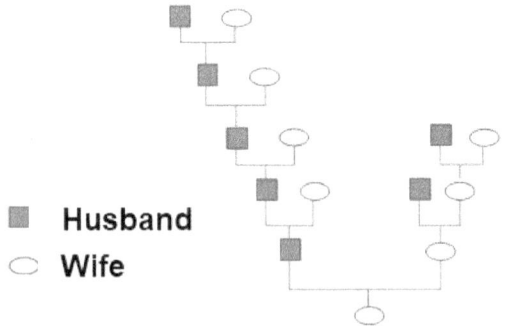

Figure: Illustration of a sapinda relationship (related within 7 generations)

1.3 Ceremonial Requirements for Marriage

The Hindu Marriage Act mandates that a Hindu marriage is a ceremonial marriage. It must be solemnized following the customary rites and ceremonies of one of the parties. If these ceremonies are not performed, the marriage may not be considered legally valid.

Special Marriage Act: Unlike the Hindu Marriage Act, the Special Marriage Act does not require any specific ceremonial rites.

1.4 Registration of a Marriage

To register a marriage under the Hindu Marriage Act or the Special Marriage Act, the parties must provide the following documents to the registrar:

- Wedding invitation, wedding photo
- Identity proof of both parties
- Address proof of both parties
- Date of birth proof of both the parties
- Certificate from priest or religious teacher
- Affidavit signed by both parties
- Passport sized photos of both parties
- A filled application form
- User fees and charges, if any are applicable in that state where marriage registration is done.

After the registrar verifies all the documents in the presence of the parties, he issues the marriage registration certificate.

A sample marriage registration certificate is shown in Fig. 2 and a sample wedding invitation card in Fig. 3.

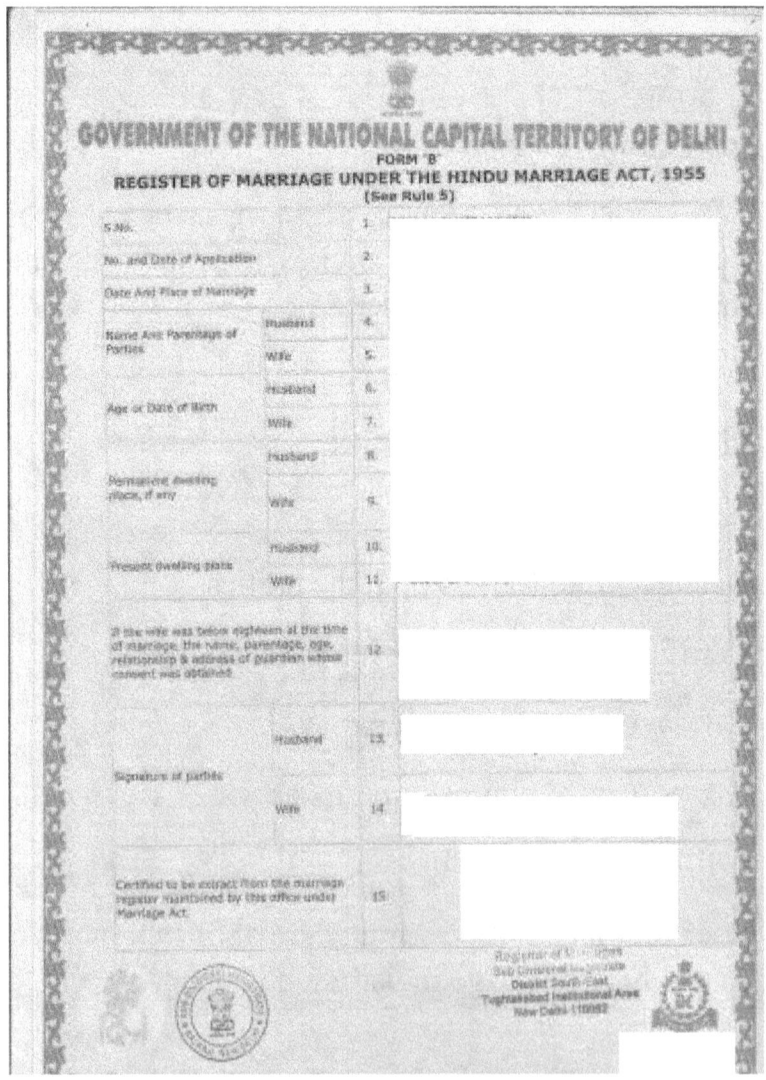

Figure: A sample marriage registration certificate

Mr. ___ and Mrs. ___
Request your presence and blessings
At the Most Auspicious Occasion
Of the Wedding Ceremony of their Nephew

Groom
Son of __ and __

to

Bride
Daughter of __ and __

On Sunday 27 February 2022
At ___

All are Welcome

Figure: A sample wedding invitation card for a Hindu wedding

THE SPECIAL MARRIAGE ACT, 1954

ACT No. 43 OF 1954[1]

[9th October, 1954.]

An Act to provide a special form of marriage in certain cases, for the registration of such and certain other marriages and for divorce.

BE it enacted by Parliament in the Fifth Year of the Republic of India as follows:—

CHAPTER I

PRELIMINARY

1. Short title, extent and commencement.—(1) This Act may be called the Special Marriage Act, 1954.

(2) It extends to the whole of India except the State of Jammu and Kashmir, and applies also to citizens of India domiciled in the territories to which this Act extends who are [2][in the State of Jammu and Kashmir].

(3) It shall come into force on such date[3] as the Central Government may, by notification in the Official Gazette, appoint.

2. Definitions.—In this Act, unless the context otherwise requires,—

[4]* * * * *

(b) "degrees of prohibited relationship"-a man and any of the persons mentioned in Part I of the First Schedule and a woman and any of the persons mentioned in Part II of the said Schedule are within the degrees of prohibited relationship.

Explanation I.—Relationship includes,—

(a) relationship by half or uterine blood as well as by full blood;

(b) illegitimate blood relationship as well as legitimate;

(c) relationship by adoption as well as by blood;

and all terms of relationship in this Act shall be construed accordingly.

Explanation II.—"Full blood" and "half blood"—two persons are said to be related to each other by full blood when they are descended from a common ancestor by the same wife and by half blood when they are descended from a common ancestor but by different wives.

Explanation III.—"Uterine blood"—two persons are said to be related to each other by uterine blood when they are descended from a common ancestress but by different husbands.

Explanation IV.—In *Explanations II* and *III*, "ancestor" includes the father and "ancestress" the

Figure: Opening page of the Special Marriage Act 1954

1.5 Laws related to marriages in India: Special Marriage Act 1954

The Special Marriage Act, 1954, provides a framework for civil marriages, enabling individuals from different religions or castes to marry without converting to each other's faith. The Act also applies to those who prefer a secular marriage ceremony. The act does not specify any particular rites for the marriage.

Procedure:

- Parties must submit a notice of intended marriage to the Marriage Registrar.
- The Registrar displays the notice publicly for 30 days.
- If no objections are raised, the marriage is solemnized.

Example:

Ananya, a Hindu, and Arjun, a Christian, decide to marry under the Special Marriage Act. They follow the due procedure, ensuring their union is valid without requiring either to renounce their faith.

1.6 Summary of requirements for marriages under the Special Marriage Act 1954

The Special Marriage Act 1954 is valid for all marriages, not just Hindu marriage. It is valid for cases where the husband and wife are not of the same religion or not of the same caste.

It is even valid for registration of marriages between Indian citizens that may happen in a foreign country.

Since no religion is specified for the special marriage act, there is no legal requirement for any special marriage ceremony such as Saptapadi ritual as is needed for the Hindu Marriage Act.

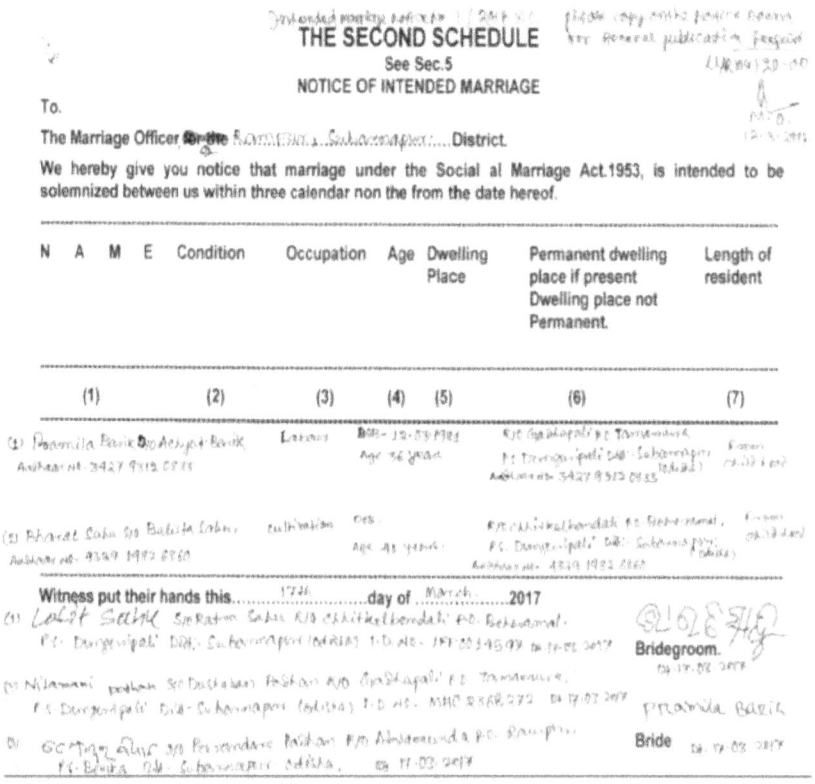

Figure: Example of a notice for marriage under the Special Marriage Act 1954

REVENUE DEPARTMENT, GOVT. OF NCT OF DELHI

APPLICATION FORM – MARRIAGE REGISTRATION CERTIFICATE

(UNDER <<THE HINDU MARRIAGE ACT, 1955>>/<<THE SPECIAL MARRIAGE ACT 1954>>/<<THE INDIAN CHRISTIAN MARRIAGE ACT, 1872>>], TheAnand Marriage Act, 1909

APPLICATNT DETAILS

1. e-DistrictRegistration Number :
   (For already Registered User- Not to be filled in by first time Applicants or those having Aadhaar number)

   OR

2. UID (AADHAAR) No :

   OR

3. Voter ID Card :
4. Name of Applicant (Bride or Groom) :

DETAILS OF GROOM AND BRIDE

		Groom	Bride
5.	Name		
6.	Father's Name		
7.	Mother's Name		
8.	Date Of Birth		
9.	Age *(as on date of marriage)*		
10.	UID (Aadhaar No)		
11.	Photo	Groom colour Passport Size Photograph Size – 5 x 4.5 (Cm.) Or 2 x 1.75 (Inch)	Bride colour Passport Size Photograph Size – 5 x 4.5 (Cm.) Or 2 x 1.75 (Inch)

12. **Address of residence in Delhi after marriage :**

House Name/No		
Sub-Locality		
Locality		
Village/Town		
Sub-division		
District		
State		
Country		
PIN Code		

Figure: Sample form for application of registration for marriage under the Special Marriage Act 1954

However, there is an additional requirement that the parties need to file a notice of intention to marry at the registrar office, at least 30 days but not more than 3 months before the actual date of marriage. This is entered into the marriage notice book, and published and open for inspection. After the expiry of 30 days, the marriage may take place. However, some third party can also file an objection to the marriage in writing before the expiry of the time period. In case of the objection, the marriage officer or registrar shall conduct a hearing and if satisfied, shall allow the marriage to take place.

As per the special marriage act, there needs to be a declaration by the parties that they are taking the other party to be their lawful wife or husband. This declaration should be made in front of the concerned officer such as registrar, along with the presence of three witnesses.

The rest of the conditions such as no living spouse at time of marriage, the minimum age of the boy (21) and girl (18) and the conditions related to mental capacity and prohibited degrees of relationship (husband and wife should not be cousins etc) remain the same as in Hindu Marriage Act.

All marriages registered under the act are entered in the marriage certificate book and can be inspected by others.

The Special Marriage Act also has sections to cover issues such as voidable marriage, child custody, alimony and divorce, similar to the Hindu Marriage Act. We discuss some of these in the following chapters of this book.

1.7 Other Personal Laws Governing Marriage in India

While this book focuses primarily on the Hindu Marriage Act and the Special Marriage Act, it is important to note that India has separate personal laws governing marriages for other religious communities.

Muslim Personal Law (Shariat) Application Act, 1937: Muslim marriages in India are governed by Muslim personal law. A Muslim marriage (Nikah) is a civil contract requiring offer (ijab) and acceptance (qubool) in the presence of two witnesses. The husband pays mehr (dower) to the wife. A Muslim husband may dissolve the marriage by talaq (divorce by the husband), while a wife may seek dissolution through khula (divorce by mutual consent at her request) or obtain a judicial dissolution under the Dissolution of Muslim Marriages Act, 1939. The Muslim Women (Protection of Rights on Divorce) Act, 1986, as interpreted by the Supreme Court, provides for maintenance of divorced Muslim women.

Indian Christian Marriage Act, 1872: Marriages among Christians in India are solemnized under this Act. The Act requires the marriage to be conducted by a Minister of Religion, a Marriage Registrar, or a person licensed to solemnize marriages. Divorce among

Christians is governed by the Indian Divorce Act, 1869 (as amended in 2001), which is discussed further in Chapter 3.

Parsi Marriage and Divorce Act, 1936: Marriages among Parsis are governed by this Act. The ceremony of Ashirvad, performed by a Parsi priest in the presence of two Parsi witnesses, is required for a valid Parsi marriage. Divorce provisions are also contained within this Act.

1.8 Conclusion

Understanding what constitutes a valid marriage is the first step in grasping the legal framework of marital relationships. However, not all marriages meet these criteria, and certain situations render a marriage invalid. In the next chapter, we will explore the conditions that make a marriage void or voidable under Indian law.

Chapter 2: What Makes a Marriage Invalid

While the law defines the conditions for a valid marriage, it also specifies circumstances under which a marriage can be considered invalid or void. This chapter explores these conditions in detail, providing insights into legal grounds that render a marriage invalid.

2.1 Conditions for validity of a marriage

The following conditions are fundamental for a marriage to be valid under the Hindu Marriage Act, 1955:

Monogamy: Neither party should have a living spouse at the time of marriage. Bigamy is strictly prohibited under the Act.

Prohibited Relationships: Parties must not fall within prohibited degrees of relationship or be sapindas of each other, unless there is a custom or usage governing both parties that permits such a marriage.

Mental Capacity: At the time of marriage, neither party should:

- Be incapable of giving valid consent due to unsoundness of mind.

- Suffer from a mental disorder that renders them unfit for marriage or procreation.
- Have recurrent episodes of insanity or epilepsy.

Minimum Age: The bridegroom must be at least 21 years old, and the bride must be at least 18 years old at the time of marriage.

Note: Child marriages are discouraged by both societal norms and legal provisions. While such marriages are punishable, they are not automatically rendered void unless specific actions are taken.

2.2 Void Marriages

A marriage is deemed void ab initio (invalid from the beginning) under the Hindu Marriage Act if it contravenes any of the following conditions:

- Either party has a living spouse at the time of the marriage (bigamy).
- The parties are within prohibited degrees of relationship.
- The parties are sapindas of each other, unless permitted by custom.

In these cases, the marriage is null and void without requiring any formal declaration by a court. However, either party may petition the court for a decree of nullity under Section 11 of the Act.

2.3 Voidable marriages

A marriage may be declared voidable under Section 12 of the Hindu Marriage Act based on specific grounds, including:

- **Impotency**: The respondent was impotent at the time of marriage and continues to be so.
- **Mental Incapacity**: At the time of marriage, the respondent was incapable of giving valid consent due to unsoundness of mind or was suffering from a mental disorder.
- **Consent Obtained by Fraud or Force**: If the consent of the petitioner or their guardian (where required) was obtained through force or fraud.
- **Pregnancy by Another Person**: At the time of marriage, the respondent was pregnant by someone other than the petitioner, and the petitioner was unaware of this fact.

Conditions for Filing:

- A petition for annulment must be filed within one year of discovering the grounds (e.g., fraud or pregnancy).

- The petitioner must not have lived with the respondent after discovering the grounds for annulment.

Example of a Void Marriage: If Ravi marries Priya while already having a legally wedded spouse, their marriage is void.

Example of a Voidable Marriage: If Priya discovers after marriage that Ravi consented to the marriage under duress, she can petition the court to declare the marriage voidable.

2.4 Conclusion

While invalid marriages are nullified outright or declared voidable, some valid marriages face challenges that lead to dissolution. In the following chapter, we delve into the legal grounds for divorce and how they provide remedies to spouses in distress.

Chapter 3: What are the Grounds for Divorce

Divorce is the legal dissolution of a valid marriage, marking the end of marital rights and obligations between the parties. It is granted by a competent court based on specific legal grounds. This chapter explores the conditions under which a divorce can be sought, distinguishing between contested divorces and divorces by mutual consent.

3.1 Grounds for Divorce under the Hindu Marriage Act, 1955

Under Section 13 of the Hindu Marriage Act, either spouse can petition for divorce on the following grounds:

- **Adultery**: When a spouse engages in sexual relations outside the marriage.

- **Cruelty**: Physical or mental cruelty inflicted by one spouse on the other.

- **Desertion**: Abandonment of one spouse by the other for a continuous period of at least two years before filing the petition.

- **Conversion**: Conversion of one spouse to another religion, ceasing to be a Hindu.

- **Mental Disorder**: If one spouse suffers from an incurable and severe mental disorder, making it unreasonable for the other spouse to live with them.

- **Leprosy**: A spouse suffering from a virulent and incurable form of leprosy.

- **Venereal Disease**: A communicable venereal disease that is incurable.

- **Renunciation**: A spouse renouncing the world by entering a religious order.

- **Presumption of Death**: If a spouse is not heard of as being alive for at least seven years, by those who would naturally have heard of them.

3.2 Additional Grounds for Divorce for Women

In addition to the grounds mentioned above, a wife may seek divorce on the following grounds under Section 13(2):

Pre-marriage Bigamy: The husband had another living wife at the time of the petitioner's marriage.

Rape, Sodomy, or Bestiality: The husband is guilty of any of these acts.

Maintenance Order: The husband has failed to comply with a court-ordered maintenance award for the wife, and cohabitation has not resumed for at least one year.

Child Marriage: The marriage occurred before the wife reached 15 years of age, and she repudiates the marriage before turning 18.

3.3 Procedure for Divorce

The steps for obtaining a divorce are as follows:

- The aggrieved party, either the husband or wife, files a petition in court citing one or more valid grounds.
- The court follows the normal legal procedure, including arguments, evidence presentation, and cross-examination.
- Based on the findings, the court may or may not grant a divorce.

Alternatively, the husband and wife may reach an agreement and apply for divorce with mutual consent rather than a contested divorce. The mutual consent divorce process is faster and less contentious than a contested divorce process, which can take years.

Figure: First page of the divorce act 1869,

3.4 Divorce Act 1869

The Divorce Act 1869 lays out the grounds for divorce. Similar grounds are also shown in the Hindu Marriage Act. The Indian Divorce Act, 1869 primarily governs divorce and matrimonial matters for Christians in India. Key grounds for divorce under this Act include adultery, conversion from Christianity, unsoundness of mind for at least two years, leprosy, venereal disease in a communicable form, and desertion for a minimum of two years. A wife may additionally seek divorce if the husband has been guilty of rape, sodomy, or bestiality. The Act was significantly amended by the Indian Divorce (Amendment) Act, 2001, which introduced mutual consent divorce for Christians (Section 10A) and removed the earlier gender discrimination in divorce proceedings. Before the 2001 amendment, women had a much higher burden of proof than men, a provision that was widely criticized. The amendment brought Christian divorce law closer to the standards of the Hindu Marriage Act and Special Marriage Act.

3.5 Grounds for annulment of marriage

The grounds for annulment include:

- Bigamy
- Fraud or coercion
- Mental incapacity

Example: Asha discovers her husband was already married. Under the Hindu Marriage Act, she can seek annulment based on bigamy.

3.6 Conclusion

Divorce is not only about identifying grounds but also about navigating the legal process and understanding options like mutual consent or contested divorce. The next chapter explores the different aspects of divorce and separation, including the processes and challenges involved.

Chapter 4: Aspects of Divorce and Separation

In this chapter, we explore key legal aspects of divorce and separation, including mutual consent divorces, judicial separation, and contested divorces.

4.1 Divorce by mutual consent

The court may grant a divorce by mutual consent under Section 13B of the Hindu Marriage Act, as amended in 1976.

The section states:

(1) Subject to the provisions of this Act a petition for dissolution of marriage by a decree of divorce may be presented to the district court by both the parties to a marriage together, whether such marriage was solemnized before or after the commencement of the Marriage Laws (Amendment) Act, 1976 (68 of 1976)*, on the ground that they have been living separately for a period of one year or more, that they have not been able to live together and that they have mutually agreed that the marriage should be dissolved.

(2) On the motion of both the parties made not earlier than six months after the date of the presentation of the petition referred to in sub-section (1) and not later than eighteen months after the said date, if the petition is not withdrawn in the meantime, the court shall, on being satisfied, after hearing the parties and after making such inquiry as it thinks fit, that a marriage has been solemnized and that the averments in the petition are true, pass a decree of divorce declaring the marriage to be dissolved with effect from the date of the decree.]

In a divorce by mutual consent, both the parties have to file an application before the court stating the circumstances of marriage, the fact that the parties have been living separately for some time, the fact that the marriage has broken down irretrievably and hence they wish to apply for a divorce. The application may also include an appendix with mutually agreed terms and conditions for the divorce.

Normally, upon receipt of an application for divorce by mutual consent, the court grants the parties a period of minimum 6 months to attempt to make up and save the marriage. The court may also propose mediation or counselling between the parties. The next hearing is held after the minimum period of 6 months. At the hearing, the judge questions both the parties to be satisfied that the marriage is truly broken down and they are applying for divorce out of their free will without any coercion, and if so, grants the decree of divorce. In certain cases, the mandatory waiting period of 6 months might be waived by the court as per its discretion.

The steps for getting a divorce by mutual consent are as follows:

- First of all, the husband and wife need to negotiate and agree on a common set of terms and conditions for the divorce. This includes how to split their assets, return of streedhan or jewellery belonging to the wife and withdrawal of any matrimonial related cases if running, how much to pay alimony, where the kids will spend their time with the parents and so on.

- Once the terms and conditions are mutually agreed, the husband and wife have to file the MCD application along with the signed agreement copy in the court.

- Normally the court gives a minimum time period of 6 months before the date of the hearing, to give the couple time to heal their differences.

- On the court hearing date after 6 months, the judge questions both the husband and wife to make sure they both want the divorce of their own free will and to be satisfied that the marriage cannot be saved. Once he is satisfied, the judge grants the MCD and the divorce process is now complete.

Divorce by mutual consent is one of the most preferred ways to get divorce, and saves the parties having to undergo many years of contentious litigation for a contested divorce, costing a lot of wasted money, time and effort.

A sample petition for divorce by mutual consent is as follows:

IN THE FAMILY COURT AT <location>

PETITION No.   / 2022

IN THE MATTER OF

NAME : AGE   : OCCUPATION : ADDRESS : Mobile No.: Email ID .... (PETITIONER NO. 1)

NAME : AGE   : OCCUPATION : ADDRESS : Mobile No.: Email ID .... (PETITIONER NO. 2)

A Petition For divorce by mutual consent U/s

(SPECIFY UNDER WHICH ACT, whether)

U/S 13B Of Hindu Marriage Act Or U/S 28 Of Special Marriage Act Or U/S 10 A Of Divorce Act

The petitioner above named submits this petition praying to state as follows;

1. That the petitioners were married to each other at ………………….. on

dated............................ according to the..............................rites and customs/ceremonies.

Or before the Marriage Registrar ....(Name of City/Town)

2. That the petitioner no. 1 before marriage was ....and petitioner no. 2 was ....

<State the pre marital status of the parties whether bachelor/ spinster/ divorcee/ widow/ widower>

<Mention the maiden name of the wife.>

<Mention the religion and domicile of the parties>

<Clearly mention the date since when the parties are staying separately>

<State the number of children. Their names and age/ date of birth and custody.>

4. State the details about pending litigation. Under which section, Act, case number and court. Next date fixed before the competent court.

5. State the details about joint immovable property, if any.

6. CONSENT TERMS

The consent terms must include what the parties decided about

The permanent alimony,

Custody and access of children,

Division of property/ execution of any registered document in respect of

immovable property Exchange of articles/jewellery/utensils etc,

Withdrawal of pending litigations, and

Any other term to which the parties are consenting)

7. That the petitioners due hereby declare and confirm that this petition preferred by them is not collusive.

8. That there is no coercion, force, fraud, undue influence, misrepresentation etc. in filing the present petition, and our consent is free.

9. That there is no collusion or connivance between the parties in filing this petition.

10. That this Court has jurisdiction to try and decide this petition as

<Mention clearly how this court has jurisdiction>

<Whether the marriage was solemnized at the location of the court>

<That the parties lastly stayed together at the location>

<The wife is staying at the location>

<Any other reason supported by document>

11. That the court fee of Rs. .... is affixed.

12. The petitioners will rely upon the documents, a list whereof is annexed herewith.

13. The petitioners pray that;

a) This Hon'ble court be pleased to dissolve the marriage between the petitioners, solemnized on .... by the decree of divorce by mutual consent under section ....

b) Such other and further relief's as this Hon'ble Court may deem fit and proper in the nature and circumstances of the case.

IN THE COURT OF :
DECREE SHEET IN PETITION FOR DIVORCE /
CONJUGAL RIGHTS / PERMANENT ALIMONY
(ORDER XX RULE 7 OF THE CODE OF CIVIL PROCEDURES)
PETITION NO

Petitioner No.1

AND

Petitioner no. 2

Claim for U/s 13B (2) of Hindu Marriage Act.
Plaint presented on 23-03-2011
This petition coming on this day for final disposal before me in the presence of :-
Sh. Tapan Choudhary Ld. counsel for petitioner no1.
Sh. Tapan Choudhary Ld. counsel for petitioner no2.

It is ordered that the marriage between the petitioner no1. and petitioner no 2. is hereby dissolved by a decree of divorce by mutual consent U/s 13-B (2) of Hindu Marriage Act. Both the petitioners shall remain bound by their respective undertakings.

And it is further ordered that the parties shall bear their own cost.

COST OF PROCEEDINGS

S.NO.	PETITION	RS.	S.NO.	RESPONDENT	RS.
	Stamps for petitioner		1.	Stamps for exhibits	
1.	Do for power		2.	Do for petition	
2.	Do for exhibits		3.	Advocate fee	
3.	Advocate fee		4.	Substance fee Wits	
4.	Substance for process		5.	Misc.	
5.	Publication fee				
6.	Service for process				
7.	Misc.				
	Total	Rs.			Rs.

Given under my hand and seal of this Court on :

DDL. DISTRICT & SESSIONS JUDGE

Figure: Sample decree of divorce by mutual consent as per section 13B of the Hindu Marriage Act

4.2 Duty of the court before grant of divorce

The court has a duty to attempt reconciliation between the parties wherever possible.

It is the duty of the court to see that the petitioner is not taking any advantage of his or her own wrongdoing. The court also has to satisfy itself that the evidence does not disclose any statutory bar or connivance, condonation, collusion, unnecessary delay in instituting proceedings or any other legal ground why divorce should not be granted, even though the matrimonial offence on the part of the other spouse may have been proved (Section 23).

4.3 Judicial separation

Judicial separation is a legal decree allowing spouses to live separately without dissolving the marriage. It provides time for introspection and potential reconciliation.

Grounds of Judicial Separation: A decree of judicial separation can be obtained by either party to marriage on any of the grounds mentioned in subsection 1 of S13, and furthermore, in case of the wife, on any of the grounds mentioned in subsection 2 of that section which relate to divorce. Therefore, the conditions for grant of judicial separation between a husband and wife are the same as the conditions for grant of divorce.

After the amending act of 1976, a party may claim only judicial separation instead of a divorce, since the grounds for both are now the same.

- Monogamy (section 17)
- Bigamy (section 17)
- Condition requirement of valid Hindu Section 5, section 7
- Relief by way of judicial separation section 10-13
- Legitimacy of children section 16
- Provision of alimony/ p.m. alimony- section 24 / section 25

4.4 Contested divorce

In a contested divorce, one spouse files for divorce without the consent of the other. These cases can take several years in Indian courts (such as 5 years or more) due to the legal complexities involved.

The grounds for a contested divorce have been covered earlier in this book. They include:

- Cruelty
- Adultery
- Desertion

- Mental disorder
- Leprosy
- Venereal disease
- Conversion to another religion
- Presumption of death

The onus is on the petitioner party to prove that one of the above grounds mentioned has been met.

4.5 Irretrievable breakdown or estrangement

Although not explicitly covered under the Hindu Marriage Act or Special Marriage Act, courts in India have occasionally granted divorces on the grounds of irretrievable breakdown of marriage. This applies when the marital bond is beyond repair, even without a specific fault by either party.

Since some time now, courts in India have come to accept the irretrievable breakdown of marriage as a concept.

However, there are also important judgments against the use of irretrievable breakdown of marriage as a ground for divorce. An example is Supreme Court of India 2009, Anil Kumar vs Maya. As per the exercise of Extraordinary jurisdiction by Supreme Court under article 142 of the Constitution of India: irretrievable breakdown of marriage is not a ground under section 13 or 13b for grant of divorce.

4.6 Restitution of Conjugal Rights (RCR)

The restitution of Conjugal Rights is applied in the case when either of the parties, whether husband or wife, has deserted from the other without a good reason and the other party wants to petition the court to bring them back. It is covered by Section 9 of the Hindu Marriage Act.

For this, either party has to file a petition for RCR before the court. It is a civil case and the normal procedure of court hearings takes place. If it is passed, the court may order the party to live with the petitioner. However, here too it is non-binding and no court can force a party to have consummation of marriage.

If one of the parties, husband or wife, wins the RCR case and the other party still does not agree to join, the party is entitled to file for divorce within one year.

4.7 Conclusion

While legal procedures define the dissolution of marriage, certain circumstances, such as mental health conditions, add complexity to divorce cases.

In the next chapter, we examine how schizophrenia and other mental disorders are addressed as grounds for divorce under Indian law.

Chapter 5: Schizophrenia and Mental Disorders as a Ground for Divorce

In this chapter, we focus on schizophrenia and other mental disorders as valid grounds for divorce under Indian marriage laws. Courts carefully evaluate evidence and legal criteria before granting divorce on these grounds.

5.1 What is Mental Disorder and Psychopathic Disorder

The expression "mental disorder" includes mental illnesses, incomplete mental development, psychopathic disorders, or other disabilities of the mind, such as schizophrenia.

Psychopathic Disorder: A persistent disorder of the mind resulting in abnormal aggression or irresponsible behaviour, whether or not medical treatment is possible.

5.2 What is Schizophrenia

Schizophrenia is a term that includes the illnesses in all age groups, which are categorized from the outset by fundamental disturbances in personality, thinking, emotional life, behaviours, interests and relationships with other people.

Its clinical features include:

- Withdrawal from social interactions
- Disordered thinking
- Emotional disconnection
- Paranoid tendencies
- Perceptual abnormalities

Case Reference: In Rameshwar Gupta vs Ram Narayan Gupta (1987), schizophrenia was recognized as a valid ground for divorce due to the severe impact on marital life.

Schizophrenia is a serious mental disorder marked by irrational thinking, disturbing emotions and breakdown of communication with others. Out of four types of this illness, namely (i) simple schizophrenia, (ii) hebephrenia, (iii) catatonia and (iv) paranoid schizophrenia, it is only the third variety in which the patient is in a state of wild excitement and destructive, violent and abusive [Rameshwar Gupta vs Ram Narayan Gupta 1987 Allahabad LR 64].

Schizophrenia is a type of mental illness and is a form of psychosis that is more serious than other types of mental illness [Rohani versus Union of India 1995 MPLJ 268, 275]

It is a mental disorder, an illness of slow insidious onset developing over years. There may be reports of strange, odd and inappropriate behaviour. There will be a progressive deterioration in the level of performance at work and school socially, examination results and employment records might provide objective and usually reliable indications of intellectual performance, its maintenance and decline [Rita Roy versus Hitesh AIR 1982 Calcutta 136]

5.3 Consequence of schizophrenia or mental disorder in a marriage

A marriage can be dissolved by a decree of divorce under Section 13(i)(iii) of the Hindu Marriage Act or Section 27(1e) of the Special Marriage Act if one spouse suffers from schizophrenia or a severe mental disorder.

Example: In Suvarna Lata vs Mohan Anand Rao (AIR 2010 SC 1586), the court granted divorce to the husband based on the wife's mental disorder.

5.4 Proof of schizophrenia or other mental disorders

To prove schizophrenia or other mental disorders, the following evidence can be presented:

- Medical prescriptions for psychiatric treatment. For example, Triperidol - is given in case of acute and chronic psychosis and psychotic disorders, mania, paranoid schizophrenia as per medical advice.

- Any other commonly prescribed medicine for schizophrenia or other psychiatric disorders may be shown.

- Records of the person visiting a psychiatrist or being prescribed brain scans can also be given as supporting evidence.

- Behavioural symptoms of the disorder, as documented by witnesses

- A positive diagnosis of schizophrenia from a doctor or medical practitioner can be shown.

5.5 Conclusion

Mental health issues can strain marriages and provide valid grounds for divorce, but they are not the only form of cruelty. Mental cruelty, encompassing emotional and psychological harm, is another critical ground for divorce. The next chapter focuses on understanding mental cruelty in the context of Indian matrimonial law.

Chapter 6: Mental Cruelty as a Ground for Divorce

Cruelty, especially mental cruelty, is a significant ground for divorce in India. It encompasses actions or behaviour that cause emotional or psychological harm to one spouse, making marital life unbearable.

6.1 Legal Perspective on Mental Cruelty

Mental cruelty is often more damaging than physical harm. It includes wilful conduct that causes suffering, apprehension, or harm to the mental or physical well-being of the spouse. Courts determine mental cruelty based on:

- The entire matrimonial relationship
- Social, cultural, and economic conditions of the parties
- Modern societal expectations and values

Mental Cruelty is to be determined on whole facts of the case and the matrimonial relations between the spouses. To amount to cruelty, there must be such wilful treatment of the party which caused suffering in body or mind, either as an actual fact or by way of apprehension, in such a manner so as to render the continued living together of spouses harmful or injurious having regard to the circumstances of the case.

The word "cruelty" has not been defined precisely and it has been used in relation to human conduct in relation to or in respect of matrimonial duties and obligations. It is a course of conduct and one which is adversely affecting the other. The cruelty may be mental or physical, intentional or unintentional.

The cruelty alleged may largely depend upon the type of life the parties are accustomed to or their economic or social conditions, their culture and human values to which they attach importance, judged by the standard of modern civilization in the background of the cultural heritage and traditions of our society.

No uniform standard can be laid down for guidance of what is meant by mental cruelty in matrimonial matters. the concept of mental cruelty cannot remain static, it is bound to change with the passage of time. what is cruelty in one case may not amount to cruelty in another case. Hence, there can never be in straitjacket formula or fixed parameters for determining what is mental cruelty in matrimonial matters.

However, there are some instances of human behaviour which may be relevant in dealing with the case of mental cruelty.

6.2 Examples of mental cruelty

The following behaviours may constitute mental cruelty:

- Sustained abusive or humiliating treatment
- Sustained neglect, indifference, or deliberate avoidance
- Persistent rudeness, coldness, or lack of affection
- Refusal to have children or unilateral decisions about sterilization
- Long periods of separation leading to irreparable marital breakdown
- On consideration of complete matrimonial life of the parties, acute mental pain, agony and suffering has would not make it possible for the parties to live with each other, could come within the broad parameters of mental cruelty
- On comprehensive appraisal of the entire matrimonial life of the parties, it becomes evidently clear that the situation is such that the wrong party cannot reasonably be asked to put up with such conduct and continue to live with the other party
- Mere coldness or lack of affection cannot amount to cruelty. frequent rudeness of language, petulance of manner, indifference and neglect may

be such a degree that it makes the married life for the other spouse absolutely intolerable

- Mental cruelty is a state of mind. The feeling of anguish, disappointment, frustration in one spouse caused by the conduct of another for a long time main lead to mental cruelty.

- Sustained unjustifiable conduct and behaviour of one spouse actually affecting the physical and mental health of the other spouse. The treatment complained of and the resultant danger of apprehension must be very grave, substantial and weighty.

- Sustained reprehensible conduct, studied neglect Indifference total departure from the normal standard of conjugal kindness causing injury to mental health or deriving sadistic pleasure can also amount to mental cruelty

- The conduct must be much more than jealousy possessive causes and happiness and dissatisfaction and emotional upset may not be a ground for grant of divorce on the ground mental cruelty

- Mere trivial irritations, quarrels, what is normal wear and tear of a married life happens in day to day life would not be adequate for grant of divorce on the ground of mental cruelty

- The married life should be reviewed as a whole and a few isolated instances over a period of years will not amount to cruelty. The ill conduct must be persistent for a fairly lengthy period, where the relationship has deteriorated to an extent that because of the acts and behaviour of a spouse, the wronged party finds it extremely difficult to live with the other party any longer, may amount to mental cruelty

- If a husband submits himself for an operation of sterilization without medical reasons and without the consent or knowledge of his wife, and similarly the wife undergoes tubectomy or abortion without medical reasons or without the consent or knowledge of her husband, such an act of the spouse may lead to mental cruelty.

- Unilateral decision of refusal to have intercourse for a considerable period without there being any physical incapacity or valid reason may amount to mental cruelty.

- Unilateral decision of either husband or wife after marriage not to have children from the marriage may amount to cruelty

- Where there has been a long period of continuous separation, it may fairly be concluded that the matrimonial bond is beyond repair. The marriage becomes a fiction supported by a legal lie. By refusing to sever that lie, the law in such cases does not serve the sanctity of the marriage. On the contrary if shows scant regard for the feelings and emotions of the parties. In such situations, it may lead to mental cruelty.

6.3 Consequence of mental cruelty being proven in a matrimonial case

When proven, mental cruelty serves as a valid ground for divorce. Courts ensure that the evidence supports the claim and consider the long-term impact on the aggrieved spouse.

6.4 Some case judgments related to mental cruelty

Below we study a few important case judgments related to cruelty:

Case 1:

Smt. Sudha vs Suhas (AIR 2005 BOM 62): Nullity of marriage granted due to epilepsy causing cruelty.

- Decree of nullity passed under section 5(ii)(c) since the appellant was suffering from 'Epilepsy' – a nervous disease in which the patient falls to the ground unconscious, with spasms and foaming at mouth.

- Section 25: the alimony has to be paid at the time of passing of final decree. Relied on the decision in the case of Shantaram v Dagubai, AIR 1987 BOM 182.

Case 2:

GVN Kumareshwara vs G Jabili (AIR 2002 SC 576): Defined mental cruelty as behaviour causing significant mental pain or suffering, making it impossible to live together. The judgment said:

"Mental cruelty in section 13(1)(1a) can be broadly defined as that conduct which inflicts on the other party such mental pain and suffering as would make it not possible for the party to live with the other. In other words, mental cruelty must be of such a nature that the parties cannot reasonably be expected to live together. The situation must be such that the wronged party cannot reasonably be asked to put up with such conduct and continue to live with the other party. It is not necessary to prove that the mental cruelty is such as to cause injury to the health of the petitioner. While arriving at such conclusion, regard must be had to the social status, education level of the parties, the society they move in, the possibility or otherwise of the parties even living together in case there already living apart, and all other relevant facts and circumstances which it is neither possible nor desirable to set out exhaustively. What is cruelty in one case may not amount to cruelty in another case. It is a matter to be determined in each case having regard to the facts and circumstances of that case. If it is a case of accusations and allegations regard must also be had to the context in which they were made".

6.5 Conclusion

Mental cruelty can make it impossible for spouses to continue their relationship. However, other factors like domicile and property rights also play crucial roles in matrimonial cases. In the next chapter, we discuss how domicile impacts legal jurisdiction and how property is divided during divorce proceedings.

Chapter 7: Domicile for matrimonial cases and division of property

This chapter explores the concept of domicile as it pertains to jurisdiction in matrimonial cases and the division of property between spouses in the event of divorce.

7.1 Domicile in matrimonial cases

Questions of domicile come when deciding the jurisdiction of a court when related to a marital dispute. In case the wife or husband file for divorce, separation, or domestic violence, 498a etc, the question is of whether a certain court has the jurisdiction to hear the case.

Domicile refers to the permanent residence of a person, which determines the jurisdiction of a court in marital disputes. A case can generally be filed in the court nearest to:

- The place where the couple last resided together (matrimonial home).
- The current residence of either spouse.

The generally accepted definition of domicile accepted by the Supreme Court is as follows: That place is properly the domicile of a person in which his habitation is fixed without any present intention of removing that form.

Key Legal Principle: The Supreme Court (AIR 1955 SC 36) ruled that domicile must include both physical presence (factum) and the intention to reside indefinitely (animus).

Note for Wives: A wife may petition the Supreme Court to transfer the case to a court closer to her place of residence if necessary.

7.2 Division of property

The division of property during divorce proceedings follows certain principles:

- **Joint Property**: Gifts or assets jointly owned by the couple at the time of marriage are divided equally.
- **Streedhan**: Property given specifically to the wife, such as jewellery or personal gifts, remains her sole property and must be returned to her in the event of divorce.

Precaution: To avoid later disputes or allegations of dowry harassment, it is advisable to create a signed list of all gifts received at the time of marriage.

Normally, the husband and wife should create a list of gifts presented jointly to both of them at the time of marriage by friends and relatives, and get it signed by both and two witnesses. These gifts belong jointly to both the parties and would be equally divided in case of divorce. Making such a list can be useful for avoiding later claims of dowry harassment as well.

Court judgment on disposal of property in case of divorce [AIR 1999 PSH 196 D/B/D 18/ 1999]: In any proceeding under the Hindu Marriage Act, the court may make such provisions in the decree as it deems just and proper with respect to any property presented at or about the time of marriage which may belong jointly to both the husband and the wife. The two pre conditions for starting the proceedings under S-27 of the Hindu marriage act are:

- The property should have been presented at or about the time of marriage
- It should be held jointly

S-27 uses the phrase 'properly presented at the time of marriage', which may belong jointly to both husband and wife. This section has one prerequisite the property must be connected with the marriage. Thus S-27 of the Act does not confine or restrict the jurisdiction of the matrimonial courts to deal with only the joint property of the parties which is presented at or about the time of marriage, but also permits disposal of exclusive property of the parties provided they were presented at or about the time of marriage.

There is also a concept of "streedhan", i.e. property belonging to the wife in a marriage. These include gifts specifically made to the wife before, during and after the marriage by friends and relatives. This can include items such as gifts of jewelry. In case of divorce, all such streedhan has to be given to the wife.

The streedhan gifts include the following: Gifts made to a woman before the marriage ceremony, gifts made at the bridal procession, gifts given as token of love by father-in-law and mother-in-law, gifts made by father, mother and brother.

To avoid later charges of dowry under 498a or any other risks, it is better for both parties to make a list of all gifts received at the time of marriage and get it signed by the bride and groom.

7.3 Conclusion

Jurisdiction and property division are critical legal aspects of marital disputes. However, addressing spousal abuse and harassment also requires legal intervention. The next chapter examines key laws like Section 498a and the Domestic Violence Act, which safeguard the rights of vulnerable spouses.

Chapter 8: 498a and Domestic Violence Act

This chapter discusses two key legal provisions for addressing marital disputes: Section 498a of the Indian Penal Code and the Protection of Women from Domestic Violence Act, 2005 (also known as Domestic Violence Act or DV Act). A number of filed cases in Indian courts are related to these acts, hence we are discussing these here.

8.1 Dowry Prohibition Act 1961 and 498a

Dowry is a social evil in Indian society since the wife's family may be poor and may have to go through hardships to pay the amount of dowry demanded by the husband's family. Hence, it is banned as per law. Dowry Prohibition Act 1961 is an act to outlaw the giving and taking of dowry. It states the following:

Definition of 'dowry': In this act, 'dowry' means any property or valuable security given or agreed to be given either directly or indirectly: by one party to a marriage to the other party to the marriage; or by the parents of either party to a marriage or by any other person, to either party to the marriage or to any other person; at or before or any time after the marriage in connection with the marriage of said parties but does not include dower or mahr in the case of persons to whom the Muslim Personal Law (Shariat) applies.

Explanation II.-The expression 'valuable security' has the same meaning as in Sec. 30 of the Indian Penal Code (45 of 1860). Penalty for giving or taking dowry.- (1) If any person, after the commencement of this Act, gives or takes or abets the giving or taking of dowry, he shall be punishable with imprisonment for a term which shall not be less than five years, and with the fine which shall not be less than fifteen thousand rupees or the amount of the value of such dowry, whichever is more.

8.2 498a: Cruelty Against Women

Section 498a was introduced to protect women from harassment or cruelty by their husbands or in-laws. It includes:

- **Definition of Cruelty**: Any conduct likely to drive a woman to suicide or cause grave injury to her physical or mental health.
- **Penalties**: Imprisonment of up to three years and a fine.

498a is an act originally brought additionally to curb the crime of dowry related harassment on wives by husbands and their family. It is part of the Indian Penal Code or IPC. Section 498a of the states the following:

Section 498A. Husband or relative of husband of a woman subjecting her to cruelty.

Whoever, being the husband or the relative of the husband of a woman, subjects such woman to cruelty shall be punished with imprisonment for a term which may extend to three years and shall also be liable to fine. Explanation.—For the purposes of this section, "cruelty means"— (a) any wilful conduct which is of such a nature as is likely to drive the woman to commit suicide or to cause grave injury or danger to life, limb or health (whether mental or physical) of the woman; or (b) harassment of the woman where such harassment is with a view to coercing her or any person related to her to meet any unlawful demand for any property or valuable security or is on account of failure by her or any person related to her to meet such demand.]

Although the original 498a act was brought to curb dowry related harassment specifically, it has been used in a number of cases wherever there is a marital dispute. There have been widespread allegations by civil society activists that this law is being misused. Often, upon mere allegations by the wife and without a proper investigation by the police, the entire family including aged parents and other relatives of the husband may get arrested on suspicion of dowry harassment. The number of 498a cases filed is high and the conviction rate is low. As per the NCRB or National Crime Records Bureau data, the number of 498a cases registered in 2020 was 111549, and only 3425 cases resulted in convictions. 120306 people were arrested, including 96497 males and 23809 females in 2020. Even the Hon. Supreme Court of India has termed the misuse of the law as "legal terrorism".

8.3 Protection of Women from Domestic Violence Act 2005 or DV Act

The Protection of Women from Domestic Violence Act, 2005 is an act to protect women who suffer from domestic violence, especially from the husband's family.

The Domestic Violence Act provides comprehensive protection to women facing various forms of abuse, including:

Types of Abuse: Physical, verbal, economic, or sexual.

Relief Measures:

- Protection orders to prevent further harm.
- Monetary relief for maintenance or medical expenses.
- Custody orders for children.
- Residence orders ensuring the woman's right to stay in the shared household.

As per this act, the wife can lodge a case and obtain protection from the court against the abuse. This can include protection, child custody, monthly maintenance being paid as well as a right to stay in the husband's shared household. This act is often used in conjunction with the 498a Act.

Key Point: While these laws provide essential safeguards, awareness and balanced implementation are necessary to ensure justice for all parties involved.

References

National Crime Records Bureau. Crime in India 2020. https://ncrb.gov.in/en/Crime-in-India-2020

https://mensdayout.com/ncrb-report-2020-crimes-against-women-cases-registered-v-s-false-conviction-vs-acquittal/

8.4 Conclusion

Marriage laws in India aim to balance fairness and justice, but their effectiveness depends on awareness and proper implementation. As we conclude, the final chapter provides a summary of key takeaways and emphasizes the evolving nature of marriage laws in India.

Chapter 9: Conclusion

This book has introduced the marriage laws in India and provided an overview of various aspects of divorce, separation, and related legal matters. By understanding these laws, individuals can better navigate their marital rights and responsibilities.

We have covered what is a valid and invalid marriage as per the Hindu Marriage Act, what are the different types of divorce, and what is the procedure for a divorce.

9.1 Key Takeaways

Marriage Laws in India: Marriage is both a social and legal institution, governed by acts such as the Hindu Marriage Act and the Special Marriage Act.

Divorce Grounds: Various grounds for divorce, including mental cruelty, desertion, and mental disorders, offer pathways to legal dissolution of marriage.

Legal Safeguards for Women: Laws like Section 498a and the Domestic Violence Act protect women from abuse and harassment.

Property and Domicile: Understanding property rights and jurisdiction is crucial in matrimonial cases.

Marriage laws in India are a blend of tradition and modernity, ensuring fairness and equality in marital relationships. This book has explored key aspects of these laws, from the conditions for valid marriages to the legal provisions for divorce, annulment, and maintenance. By understanding these laws, individuals can navigate their marital rights and responsibilities more effectively.

As societal norms evolve, so must our understanding and application of marriage laws. Awareness and advocacy are crucial for ensuring that these laws serve the purpose of protecting the institution of marriage while safeguarding individual rights.

Appendix A

THE HINDU MARRIAGE ACT, 1955

Act No. 25 of 1955 [18th May, 1955.]
An act to amend and codify the law relating to marriage among Hindus.
BE it enacted by Parliament in the Sixth Year of the Republic of India as follows:—

PRELIMINARY
1. **Short title and extent**.— This Act may be called the Hindu Marriage Act, 1955.
(2) It extends to the whole of India, and applies also to Hindus domiciled in the territories to
which this Act extends who are outside the said territories.
2. **Application of Act**—This Act applies—
(a) to any person who is a Hindu by religion in any of its forms or developments, including a Virashaiva, a Lingayat or a follower of the Brahmo, Prarthana or Arya Samaj,
(b) to any person who 1s a Buddhist, Jaina or Sikh by religion, and
(c) to any other person domiciled in the territories to which this Act extends who is not a Muslim, Christian, Parsi or Jew by religion, unless it is proved that any such person would not have been governed by the Hindu law or by any custom or usage as part of that law in respect of any of the matters dealt with herein if this Act had not been passed.
Explanation.—The following persons are Hindus, Buddhists, Jainas or Sikhs by religion, as the case may be:—
(a) any child, legitimate or illegitimate, both of whose parents are Hindus, Buddhists, Jainas or Sikhs by religion;
(b) any child, legitimate or illegitimate, one of whose parents is a Hindu, Buddhist, Jaina or Sikh by religion and who is brought up as a member of the tribe, community, group or family to which such parent belongs or belonged; and

(c) any person who is a convert or re-convert to the Hindu, Buddhist, Jaina or Sikh religion.

(2) Notwithstanding anything contained in sub-section, nothing contained in this Act shall apply to the members of any Scheduled tribe within the meaning of clause (25) of article 366 of the Constitution unless the Central Government, by notification in the Official Gazette, otherwise directs.

(3) The expression "Hindu" in any portion of this Act shall be construed as if it included a person who, though not a Hindu by religion, is, nevertheless, a person to whom this Act applies by virtue of the provisions contained in this section.

3. **Definitions**.—In this Act, unless the context otherwise requires,—

(a) the expressions "custom" and "usage" signify any rule which, having been continuously and uniformly observed for a long time, has obtained the force of law among Hindus in any local area, tribe, community, group or family:

Provided that the rule is certain and not unreasonable or opposed to public policy; and

Provided further that in the case of a rule applicable only to a family it has not been discontinued by the family;

(6) "district court" means, in any area for which there is a city civil court, that court, and in any other area the principal civil court of original jurisdiction, and includes any other civil court which may be specified by the State Government, by notification in the Official Gazette, as having jurisdiction in respect of the matters dealt with in this Act;

(c) "full blood" and "half blood"—two persons are said to be related to each other by full blood when they are descended from a common ancestor by the same wife and by half blood when they are

descended from a common ancestor but by different wives;

(d) "uterine blood'"—two persons are said to be related to each other by uterine blood when they are descended from a common ancestress but by different husbands;

Explanation.—In clauses (c) and (d), "ancestor" includes the father and "ancestress" the mother,

(e) "prescribed" means prescribed by rules made under this Act;

(f) "sapinda relationship" with reference to any person extends as far as the third generation (inclusive) in the line of ascent through the mother, and the fifth (inclusive) in the line of ascent through the father, the line being traced upwards in each case from the person concerned, who 1s to be counted as the first generation;

(ii) two persons are said to be "sapindas" of each other if one is a lineal ascendant of the other within the limits of sapinda relationship, or if they have a common lineal ascendant who is within the limits of sapinda relationship with reference to each of them;

(g) "degrees of prohibited relationship'-two persons are said to be within the "degrees of prohibited relationship"—

(i) if one 1s a lineal ascendant of the other; or

(ii) if one was the wife or husband of a lineal ascendant or descendant of the other; or

(iii) 1f one was the wife of the brother or of the father's or mother's brother or of the grandfather's or grandmother's brother of the other; or

(iv) if the two are brother and sister, uncle and niece, aunt and nephew, or children of brother and sister or of two brothers or of two sisters;

Explanation.—For the purposes of clauses (/) and (g), relationship includes—

(i) relationship by half or uterine blood as well as by full blood;

(ii) illegitimate blood relationship as well as legitimate;

(iit) relationship by adoption as well as by blood;

and all terms of relationship in those clauses shall be construed accordingly.

4. **Overriding effect of Act**—Save as otherwise expressly provided in this Act,—

(a) any text rule or interpretation of Hindu law or any custom or usage as part of that law in force immediately before the commencement of this Act shall cease to have effect with respect to any matter for which provision is made in this Act;

(6) any other law in force immediately before the commencement of this Act shall cease to have effect in so far as it is inconsistent with any of the provisions contained in this Act.

HINDU MARRIAGES

5. **Conditions for a Hindu marriage.**—A marriage may be solemnized between any two Hindus, if the following conditions are fulfilled, namely:—

(i) neither party has a spouse living at the time of the marriage; i.e at the time of the marriage, neither party—

(a) is incapable of giving a valid consent to it in consequence of unsoundness of mind; or

(b) though capable of giving a valid consent, has been suffering from mental disorder of such a kind or to such an extent as to be unfit for marriage and the procreation of children; or

(c) has been subject to recurrent attacks of insanity

(iii) the bridegroom has completed the age of 21 [twenty-one years] and the bride, the age of 18 [eighteen years] at the time of the marriage;

(iv) the parties are not within the degrees of prohibited relationship unless the custom or usage governing each of them permits of a marriage between the two;

(v) the parties are not sapindas of each other, unless the custom or usage governing each of them permits of a marriage between the two;

6. **Guardianship in marriage.**|—Omitted by the Child Marriage Restraint (Amendment) Act, 1978, (2 of 1978), s. 6 and Schedule (w.e.f. 1-10-1978).

7. **Ceremonies for a Hindu marriage**— A Hindu marriage may be solemnized in accordance with the customary rites and ceremonies of either party thereto.

(2) Where such rites and ceremonies include the Saptapadi (that is, the taking of seven steps by the bridegroom and the bride jointly

before the sacred fire), the marriage becomes complete and binding when the seventh step is taken.

8. **Registration of Hindu marriages**— For the purpose of facilitating the proof of Hindu marriages, the State Government may make rules providing that the parties to any such marriage may have the particulars relating to their marriage entered in such manner and subject to such conditions as may be prescribed in a Hindu Marriage Register kept for the purpose.

(2) Notwithstanding anything contained in sub-section (/), the State Government may, if it is of opinion that it is necessary or expedient so to do, provide that the entering of the particulars referred to in sub-section (/) shall be compulsory in the State or in any part thereof, whether in all cases or in such cases as may be specified, and where any such direction has been issued, any person contravening any rule made in this behalf shall be punishable with fine which may extend to twenty-five rupees.

(3) All rules made under this section shall be laid before the State Legislature, as soon as may be, after they are made.

(4) The Hindu Marriage Register shall at all reasonable times be open for inspection, and shall be admissible as evidence of the statements therein contained and certified extracts therefrom shall, on application, be given by the Registrar on payment to him of the prescribed fee.

(3) Notwithstanding anything contained in this section, the validity of any Hindu marriage shall in no way be affected by the omission to make the entry.

RESTITUTION OF CONJUGAL RIGHTS AND JUDICIAL SEPARATION

9. **Restitution of conjugal right** — When either the husband or the wife has, without reasonable excuse, withdrawn from the society of the other, the aggrieved party may apply, by petition to the district court, for restitution of conjugal rights and the court, on being satisfied of the truth of the statements made in such petition and that there is no legal ground why the application should not be granted, may decree restitution of conjugal rights accordingly.

°[Explanation—Where a question arises whether there has been reasonable excuse for withdrawal from the society, the burden of proving reasonable excuse shall be on the person who has withdrawn from the society.]

10. **Judicial separation** —Either party to a marriage, whether solemnised before or after the commencement of this Act, may present a petition praying for a decree for judicial separation on any of the grounds specified in sub-section (/) of section 13, and in the case of a wife also on any of the grounds specified in sub-section (2) thereof, as grounds on which a petition for divorce might have been presented.

(2) Where a decree for judicial separation has been passed, it shall no longer be obligatory for the petitioner to cohabit with the respondent, but the court may, on the application by petition of either party and on being satisfied of the truth of the statements made in such petition, rescind the decree if it considers it just and reasonable to do so.

NULLITY OF MARRIAGE AND DIVORCE

11. **Void marriages**.—Any marriage solemnised after the commencement of this Act shall be null and void and may, on a petition presented by either party thereto *[against the other party], be so declared by a decree of nullity if it contravenes any one of the conditions specified in clauses (i), (iv) and (v) of section 5.

12. **Voidable marriages**.—Any marriage solemnised, whether before or after the commencement of this Act, shall be voidable and may be annulled by a decree of nullity on any of the following grounds, namely:—

3[that the marriage has not been consummated owing to the impotence of the respondent; or] (6) that the marriage is in contravention of the condition specified in clause (7) of section 5; or

(c) that the consent of the petitioner, or where the consent of the guardian in marriage of the petitioner "[was required under section 5 as it stood immediately before the commencement of the Child Marriage Restraint (Amendment) Act, 1978 (2 of 1978)], the consent of such guardian was obtained by force *[or by fraud as to the nature of the ceremony or as to any material fact or circumstances concerning the respondent]; or

(d) that the respondent was at the time of the marriage pregnant by some person other than the petitioner.

(2) Notwithstanding anything contained in sub-section (/), no petition for annulling a marriage—

(a) on the ground specified in clause (c) of sub-section (/) shall be entertained if—

(i) the petition is presented more than one year after the force had ceased to operate or, as the case may be, the fraud had been discovered; or

(ii) the petitioner has, with his or her full consent, lived with the other party to the marriage as husband or wife after the force had ceased to operate or, as the case may be, the fraud had been discovered;

(6) on the ground specified in clause (d) of sub-section (/) shall be entertained unless the court is satisfied—

(i) that the petitioner was at the time of the marriage ignorant of the facts alleged;

(ii) that proceedings have been instituted in the case of a marriage solemnised before the commencement of this Act within one year of such commencement and in the case of marriages solemnised after such commencement within one year from the date of the marriage; and

(iii) that marital intercourse with the consent of the petitioner has not taken place since the discovery by the petitioner of the existence of the said ground.

13. **Divorce**- Any marriage solemnized, whether before or after the commencement of this Act, may, on a petition presented by either the husband or the wife, be dissolved by a decree of divorce on the ground that the other party—

has, after the solemnization of the marriage, had voluntary sexual intercourse with any person other than his or her spouse; or

(ia) has, after the solemnization of the marriage, treated the petitioner with cruelty; or

(ib) has deserted the petitioner for a continuous period of not less than two years immediately preceding the presentation of the petition; or]
(ii) has ceased to be a Hindu by conversion to another religion; or
7(ii) has been incurably of unsound mind, or has been suffering continuously or intermittently
from mental disorder of such a kind and to such an extent that the petitioner cannot reasonably be expected to live with the respondent.
Explanation.—In this clause,—
(a) the expression "mental disorder' means mental illness, arrested or incomplete development of mind, psychopathic disorder or any other disorder or disability of mind and includes schizophrenia;
(b) the expression "psychopathic disorder" means a persistent disorder or disability of mind (whether or not including sub—normality of intelligence) which results in abnormally aggressive or seriously irresponsible conduct on the part of the other party, and whether or not it requires or is susceptible to medical treatment; or]
(v) has been suffering from venereal disease in a communicable form; or
(vi) has renounced the world by entering any religious order; or
(vii) has not been heard of as being alive for a period of seven years or more by those persons who would naturally have heard of it, had that party been alive;
7 Explanation—In this sub-section, the expression "desertion" means the desertion of the petitioner by the other party to the marriage without reasonable cause and without the consent or against the wish of such party, and includes the wilful neglect of the petitioner by the other party to the marriage, and its grammatical variations and cognate expressions shall be construed accordingly.
8[(1A) Either party to a marriage, whether solemnized before or after the commencement of this Act, may also present a petition for the dissolution of the marriage by a decree of divorce on the ground—

(i) that there has been no resumption of cohabitation as between the parties to the marriage for a period of °[one year] or upwards after the passing of a decree for judicial separation in a proceeding to which they were parties; or

(ii) that there has been no restitution of conjugal rights as between the parties to the marriage for a period of [one year] or upwards after the passing of a decree for restitution of conjugal rights in a proceeding to which they were parties.

(2) A wife may also present a petition for the dissolution of her marriage by a decree of divorce on the ground,—

(i) in the case of any marriage solemnized before the commencement of this Act, that the husband had married again before such commencement or that any other wife of the husband married before such commencement was alive at the time of the solemnization of the marriage of the petitioner:

Provided that in either case the other wife is alive at the time of the presentation of the petition; or

(ii) that the husband has, since the solemnization of the marriage, been guilty of rape, sodomy or bestiality; or that in a suit under section 18 of the Hindu Adoptions and Maintenance Act, 1956 (78 of 1956), or in a proceeding under section 125 of the Code of Criminal Procedure, 1973 (2 of 1974) (or under the corresponding section 488 of the Code of Criminal Procedure, 1898 (5 of 1898), a decree or order, as the case may be, has been passed against the husband awarding maintenance to the wife notwithstanding that she was living apart and that since the passing of such decree or order, cohabitation between the parties has not been resumed for one year or upwards;

(iv) that her marriage (whether consummated or not) was solemnized before she attained the age of fifteen years and she has repudiated the marriage after attaining that age but before attaining the age of eighteen years.

Explanation.—This clause applies whether the marriage was solemnized before or after the commencement of the Marriage Laws (Amendment) Act, 1976 (68 of 1976).]

13A. **Alternate relief in divorce proceedings**.—In any proceeding under this Act, on a petition for dissolution of marriage by a decree of divorce, except in so far as the petition is founded on the grounds mentioned in clauses (77), (v7) and (vii) of sub-section (/) of section 13, the court may, if it considers it just so to do having regard to the circumstances of the case, pass instead a decree for judicial separation.

13B. **Divorce by mutual consent**.—Subject to the provisions of this Act a petition for dissolution of marriage by a decree of divorce may be presented to the district court by both the parties to a marriage

together, whether such marriage was solemnized before or after the commencement of the Marriage Laws (Amendment) Act, 1976 (68 of 1976), on the ground that they have been living separately for a period of one year or more, that they have not been able to live together and that they have mutually agreed that the marriage should be dissolved.

(2) On the motion of both the parties made not earlier than six months after the date of the presentation of the petition referred to in sub-section (/) and not later than eighteen months after the said date, if the petition is not withdrawn in the meantime, the court shall, on being satisfied, after hearing the parties and after making such inquiry as it thinks fit, that a marriage has been solemnized and that the averments in the petition are true, pass a decree of divorce declaring the marriage to be dissolved with effect from the date of the decree.

14. **No petition for divorce to be presented within one year of marriage**.—(/) Notwithstanding anything contained in this Act, it shall not be competent for any court to entertain any petition for

dissolution of a marriage by a decree of divorce, '[unless at the date of the presentation of the petition one year has elapsed] since the date of the marriage:

Provided that the court may, upon application made to it in accordance with such rules as may be made by the High Court in that behalf, allow a petition to be presented before one year has elapsed since the date of the marriage on the ground that the case is one of exceptional hardship to the petitioner or of exceptional depravity on the part of the respondent, but if it appears to the court at the hearing of the petition that the petitioner obtained leave to present the petition by any misrepresentation or concealment of the nature of the case, the court may, if it pronounces a decree, do so subject to the condition that the decree shall not have effect until after the expiry of one year from the date of the marriage or may dismiss the petition without prejudice to any petition which may be brought after expiration of the said one year upon the same or substantially the same facts as those alleged in support of the petition so dismissed.

(2) In disposing of any application under this section for leave to present a petition for divorce before the "[expiration of one year] from the date of the marriage, the court shall have regard to the interests of any children of the marriage and to the question whether there is a reasonable probability of a reconciliation between the parties before the expiration of the *[said one year].

15. Divorced persons when may marry again.—When a marriage has been dissolved by a decree of divorce and either there is no right of appeal against the decree or, if there is such a right of appeal, the time for appealing has expired without an appeal having been presented, or an appeal has been presented but has been dismissed, it shall be lawful for either party to the marriage to marry again.

16. Legitimacy of children of void and voidable marriages — Notwithstanding that a marriage is null and void under section 11, any child of such marriage who would have been legitimate if the marriage had been valid, shall be legitimate, whether such child is born before or after the commencement of the Marriage Laws (Amendment) Act, 1976 (68 of 1976), and whether or not a decree of nullity is granted in respect of that marriage under this Act and whether or not the marriage is held to be void otherwise than on a petition under this Act.

(2) Where a decree of nullity is granted in respect of a voidable marriage under section 12, any child begotten or conceived before the decree is made, who would have been the legitimate child of

the parties to the marriage if at the date of the decree it had been dissolved instead of being annulled, shall be deemed to be their legitimate child notwithstanding the decree of nullity.

(3) Nothing contained in sub-section (/) or sub-section (2) shall be construed as conferring upon any child of a marriage which is null and void or which 1s annulled by a decree of nullity under section 12, any rights in or to the property of any person, other than the parents, in any case where, but for the passing of this Act, such child would have been incapable of possessing or acquiring any such rights by

reason of his not being the legitimate child of his parents.

17. **Punishment of bigamy**.—Any marriage between two Hindus solemnized after the commencement of this Act is void if at the date of such marriage either party had a husband or wife living; and the provisions of sections 494 and 495 of the Indian Penal Code, 1860 (45 of 1860), shall apply accordingly.

18. **Punishment for contravention of certain other conditions for a Hindu marriage**.—Every person who procures a marriage of himself or herself to be solemnized under this Act in contravention of the conditions specified in clauses (iif), (iv), '[and (v)] of section 5 shall be punishable—

(a) in the case of contravention of the condition specified in clause (iii) of section 5, with rigorous imprisonment which may extend to two years or with fine which may extend to one lakh

rupees, or with both.

(b) in the case of a contravention of the condition specified in clause (iv) or clause (v) of section 5, with simple imprisonment which may extend to one month, or with fine which may extend to one thousand rupees, or with both

JURISDICTION AND PROCEDURE

19. **Court to which petition shall be presented**.—Every petition under this Act shall be presented to the District Court within the local limits of whose ordinary original civil jurisdiction: —

(i) the marriage was solemnized, or

(ii) the respondent, at the time of the presentation of the petition, resides, or

(iii) the parties to the marriage last resided together, or

°[(iiia) in case the wife is the petitioner, where she is residing on the date of presentation of the petition; or]

(iv) the petitioner is residing at the time of the presentation of the petition, in a case where the respondent is at that time, residing outside the territories to which this Act extends, or has not been heard of as being alive for a period of seven years or more by those persons who would naturally have heard of him if he were alive. |

20. **Contents and verification of petitions**—(/) Every petition presented under this Act shall state as distinctly as the nature of the case permits the facts on which the claim to relief is founded and, except in a petition under section 11, shall also state that there is no collusion between the petitioner and the other party to the marriage.

(2) The statements contained in every petition under this Act shall be verified by the petitioner or some other competent person in the manner required by law for the verification of plaints, and may, at the

hearing, be referred to as evidence.

21. **Application of Act 5 of 1908.**—Subject to the other provisions contained in this Act and to such rules as the High Court may make in this behalf, all proceedings under this Act shall be regulated, as far as may be, by the Code of Civil Procedure, 1908.

21A. **Power to transfer petitions in certain cases.**—Where—

(a) a petition under this Act has been presented to a district court having jurisdiction by a party to a marriage praying for a decree for judicial separation under section 10 or for a decree of divorce under section 13, and

(b) another petition under this Act has been presented thereafter by the other party to the marriage praying for a decree for judicial separation under section 10 or for a decree of divorce under section 13 on any ground, whether in the same district court or in a different district court, in the same State or in a different State, the petitions shall be dealt with as specified in sub-section (2).

(2) In a case where sub-section (J) applies,—
(a) if the petitions are presented to the same district court, both the petitions shall be tried and heard together by that district court;
(b) if the petitions are presented to different district courts, the petition presented later shall be transferred to the district court in which the earlier petition was presented and both the petitions shall be heard and disposed of together by the district court in which the earlier petition was presented.
(3) In a case where clause (b) of sub-section (2) applies, the court or the Government, as the case may be, competent under the Code of Civil Procedure, 1908 (5 of 1908), to transfer any suit or proceeding from the district court in which the later petition has been presented to the district court in which the earlier petition is pending, shall exercise its powers to transfer such later petition as if it had been empowered so to do under the said Code.

21B. **Special provision relating to trial and disposal of petitions under the Act**.—The trial of a petition under this Act shall, so far as is practicable consistently with the interests of justice in respect of
the trial, be continued from day to day until its conclusion unless the court finds the adjournment of the trial beyond the following day to be necessary for reasons to be recorded.
(2) Every petition under this Act shall be tried as expeditiously as possible and endeavour shall be made to conclude the trial within six months from the date of service of notice of the petition on the respondent.
(3) Every appeal under this Act shall be heard as expeditiously as possible, and endeavour shall be made to conclude the hearing within three months from the date of service of notice of appeal on the
respondent.

21C. **Documentary evidence**—Notwithstanding anything in any enactment to the contrary, no document shall be inadmissible in evidence in any proceeding at the trial of a petition under this Act on
the ground that it is not duly stamped or registered.]

22. **Proceedings to be in camera and may not be printed or published**.—Every proceeding under this Act shall be conducted in camera and it shall not be lawful for any person to print or publish
any matter in relation to any such proceeding except a judgment of the High Court or of the Supreme Court printed or published with the previous permission of the court.
(2) If any person prints or publishes any matter in contravention of the provisions contained in sub-section (1), he shall be punishable with fine which may extend to one thousand rupees.
23. **Decree in proceedings**.—In any proceeding under this Act, whether defended or not, if the court is satisfied that
(a) any of the grounds for granting relief exists and the petitioner *[except in cases where the relief is sought by him on the ground specified in sub-clause (a), sub-clause (6) or sub-clause (c) of clause (ii) of section 5] is not in any way taking advantage of his or her own wrong or disability for the purpose of such relief, and
(b) where the ground of the petition is the ground specified '* * * in clause (7) of sub-section (J) of section 13, the petitioner has not in any manner been accessory to or connived at or condoned the act or acts complained of, or where the ground of the petition is cruelty the petitioner has not in any manner condoned the cruelty, and
2[(bb) when a divorce is sought on the ground of mutual consent, such consent has not been obtained by force, fraud or undue influence, and]
(c) *[the petition (not being a petition presented under section 11)] is not presented or prosecuted in collusion with the respondent, and
(d) there has not been any unnecessary or improper delay in instituting the proceeding, and
(e) there is no other legal ground why relief should not be granted, then, and in such a case, but not otherwise, the court shall decree such relief accordingly.
(2) Before proceeding to grant any relief under this Act, it shall be the duty of the court in the first instance, in every case where it is possible so to do consistently with the nature and circumstances of

the case, to make every endeavour to bring about reconciliation between the parties:

3[Provided that nothing contained in this sub-section shall apply to any proceeding wherein relief is sought on any of the grounds specified in clause (ii), clause (iii), clause (iv), clause (v), clause (vi) or clause (vii) of sub-section (/) of section 13.]

71(3) For the purpose of aiding the court in bringing about such reconciliation, the court may, if the parties so desire or if the court thinks it just and proper so to do, adjourn the proceedings for a reasonable period not exceeding fifteen days and refer the matter to any person named by the parties in this behalf or to any person nominated by the court if the parties fail to name any person, with directions to report to the court as to whether reconciliation can be and has been, effected and the court shall in disposing of the proceeding have due regard to the report.

(4) In every case where a marriage is dissolved by a decree of divorce, the court passing the decree shall give a copy thereof free of cost to each of the parties.

23A. **Relief for respondent in divorce and other proceedings**.— In any proceeding for divorce or judicial separation or restitution of conjugal rights, the respondent may not only oppose the relief sought on the ground of petitioner's adultery, cruelty or desertion, but also make a counter-claim for any relief under this Act on that ground; and if the petitioner's adultery, cruelty or desertion is proved, the court may give to the respondent any relief under this Act to which he or she would have been entitled if he or she had presented a petition seeking such relief on that ground.

24. **Maintenance pendente lite and expenses of proceedings**.— Where in any proceeding under this Act it appears to the court that either the wife or the husband, as the case may be, has no independent income sufficient for her or his support and the necessary expenses of the proceeding, it may, on the application of the wife or the husband, order the respondent to pay to the petitioner the expenses of the proceeding, and monthly during the proceeding such sum as, having regard to the petitioner's own

income and the income of the respondent, it may seem to the court to be reasonable.

[Provided that the application for the payment of the expenses of the proceeding and such monthly sum during the proceeding, shall, as far as possible, be disposed of within sixty days from the date of service of notice on the wife or the husband, as the case may be.]

25. **Permanent alimony and maintenance.**—(/) Any court exercising jurisdiction under this Act may, at the time of passing any decree or at any time subsequent thereto, on application made to it for the

purpose by either the wife or the husband, as the case may be, order that the respondent shall pay to the applicant for her or his maintenance and support such gross sum or such monthly or periodical sum for a term not exceeding the life of the applicant as, having regard to the respondent's own income and other property, if any, the income and other property of the applicant '[the conduct of the parties and other circumstances of the case], it may seem to the court to be just, and any such payment may be secured, if necessary, by a charge on the immovable property of the respondent.

(2) If the court is satisfied that there is a change in the circumstances of either party at any time after it has made an order under sub-section (/), it may, at the instance of either party, vary, modify or rescind

any such order in such manner as the court may deem just.

(3) If the court is satisfied that the party in whose favour an order has been made under this section has re-married or, if such party is the wife, that she has not remained chaste, or, if such party is the husband, that he has had sexual intercourse with any woman outside wedlock, *[it may at the instance of the other party vary, modify or rescind any such order in such manner as the court may deem just].

26. **Custody of children.**—In any proceeding under this Act, the court may, from time to time, pass such interim orders and make such provisions in the decree as it may deem just and proper with respect to

the custody, maintenance and education of minor children, consistently with their wishes, wherever possible, and may, after the decree, upon application by petition for the purpose, make from time to time, all such orders and provisions with respect to the custody, maintenance and education of such children as might have been made by such decree or interim orders in case the proceeding for obtaining such decree were still pending, and the court may also from time to time revoke, suspend or vary any such orders and provisions previously made:

3[Provided that the application with respect to the maintenance and education of the minor children, pending the proceeding for obtaining such decree, shall, as far as possible, be disposed of within sixty days from the date of service of notice on the respondent.

27. **Disposal of property**.—In any proceeding under this Act, the court may make such provisions in the decree as it deems just and proper with respect to any property presented, at or about the time of
marriage, which may belong jointly to both the husband and the wife.

28. **Appeals from decrees and orders**.— All decrees made by the court in any proceeding under this Act shall, subject to the provisions of sub-section (3), be appealable as decrees of the court made in the exercise of its original civil jurisdiction, and every such appeal shall lie to the court to which appeals ordinarily lie from the decisions of the court given in the exercise of its original civil jurisdiction.

(2) Orders made by the court in any proceeding under this Act under section 25 or section 26 shall, subject to the provisions of sub-section (3), be appealable if they are not interim orders, and every such appeal shall lie to the court to which appeals ordinarily lie from the decisions of the court given in exercise of its original civil jurisdiction.

(3) There shall be no appeal under this section on the subject of costs only.

(4) Every appeal under this section shall be preferred within a period of ninety days from the date of the decree or order.

28A. **Enforcement of decrees and orders**.—All decrees and orders made by the court in any proceeding under this Act shall be enforced in the like manner as the decrees and orders of the court made in the exercise of its original civil jurisdiction for the time being in forced.

SAVINGS AND REPEALS

29. **Savings**.— A marriage solemnized between Hindus before the commencement of this Act, which is otherwise valid, shall not be deemed to be invalid or ever to have been invalid by reason only of the fact that the parties thereto belonged to the same gotra or pravara or belonged to different religions, castes or sub-divisions of the same caste.

(2) Nothing contained in this Act shall be deemed to affect any right recognised by custom or conferred by any special enactment to obtain the dissolution of a Hindu marriage, whether solemnized before or after the commencement of this Act.

(3) Nothing contained in this Act shall affect any proceeding under any law for the time being in force for declaring any marriage to be null and void or for annulling or dissolving any marriage or for judicial separation pending at the commencement of this Act, and any such proceeding may be continued and determined as if this Act had not been passed.

(4) Nothing contained in this Act shall be deemed to affect the provisions contained in the Special Marriage Act, 1954, (43 of 1954) with respect to marriages between Hindus solemnized under that Act, whether before or after the commencement of this Act.

30. **Repeals**—Rep. by the Repealing and Amending Act, 1960 (58 of 1960), s. 2 and the First Schedule (w.e.f. 26-12-1960).

Glossary of Legal Terms

This glossary defines key legal terms used throughout this book to assist readers who may be unfamiliar with legal terminology.

Adultery: Voluntary sexual intercourse between a married person and someone who is not their spouse. A ground for divorce under the Hindu Marriage Act.

Alimony / Maintenance: Financial support paid by one spouse to the other after separation or divorce. Under the Hindu Marriage Act, either spouse may apply for permanent alimony (Section 25) or interim maintenance during proceedings (Section 24).

Annulment: A legal declaration that a marriage is null and void, as if it never existed. Distinct from divorce, which ends a valid marriage.

Bigamy: The act of marrying someone while already being legally married to another person. Bigamy is an offence under Section 17 of the Hindu Marriage Act and Section 494 of the Indian Penal Code.

Decree: A formal order issued by a court. A divorce decree formally dissolves a marriage.

Desertion: Abandonment of one spouse by the other without reasonable cause and without consent, for a continuous period of at least two years. A ground for divorce under Section 13(ib) of the Hindu Marriage Act.

Domicile: The place where a person has their permanent home and to which, if absent, they intend to return. Domicile determines the jurisdiction of a court in matrimonial cases.

Dowry: Property or valuable security given or agreed to be given in connection with a marriage. Giving or taking dowry is prohibited under the Dowry Prohibition Act, 1961.

Judicial Separation: A court decree allowing spouses to live apart without dissolving the marriage. The parties remain legally married but are no longer obliged to cohabit.

Mutual Consent Divorce (MCD): A divorce obtained by agreement of both spouses, under Section 13B of the Hindu Marriage Act or Section 28 of the Special Marriage Act. It is generally faster and less contentious than a contested divorce.

Nullity of Marriage: A legal declaration that a marriage was never valid. A void marriage is automatically null; a voidable marriage must be declared null by court decree.

Petitioner: The party who files a petition or application in court seeking legal relief.

Respondent: The party against whom a petition is filed in court.

Restitution of Conjugal Rights (RCR): A legal remedy available to a spouse who has been deserted by the other, whereby the court may order the deserting spouse to return to the matrimonial home. Governed by Section 9 of the Hindu Marriage Act.

Sapinda Relationship: A relationship by lineage defined under the Hindu Marriage Act, extending up to three generations on the maternal side and five generations on the paternal side. Marriage between sapindas is prohibited unless permitted by custom.

Saptapadi: The ritual of taking seven steps around a sacred fire, performed as part of a Hindu wedding ceremony. Under Section 7(2) of the Hindu Marriage Act, where Saptapadi is observed, the marriage is complete when the seventh step is taken.

Streedhan: Property belonging exclusively to the wife, including gifts made to her before, during, and after the marriage by relatives and friends. In case of divorce, streedhan must be returned to the wife.

Void Marriage: A marriage that is invalid from the very beginning (void ab initio) and has no legal effect. Examples include bigamous marriages and marriages within prohibited degrees of relationship.

Voidable Marriage: A marriage that is valid unless annulled by a court on specific grounds, such as impotency, mental incapacity at the time of marriage, or consent obtained by fraud or force.

Acknowledgments

In writing this book, we have consulted a number of sources including the following:

Mulla Hindu Law by Sir Dinshan Firdunji Mulla: Updated 21st Edition by Satyajit A Desia, published by LexisNexis.

Universal's - The Hindu Marriage Act, 1955 as amended by the Jammu and Kashmir Reorganisation Act, 2019 and The Personal Laws (Amendment) Act, 2019

About the author

Siva Prasad Bose is a writer of guidebooks on laws in India. He currently retired after many years of service as an electrical engineer in Uttar Pradesh Power Corporation Limited (UPPCL). He received his engineering degree from Jadavpur University, Kolkata and has a law degree from Meerut University, Meerut. His interests lie in the fields of family law, civil law, law of contracts, and any areas of law related to power electricity related issues. He lives in CR Park, New Delhi with his family.

Other Books by Siva Prasad Bose

Introduction to Wills and Probate

Senior Citizens Abuse in India

Introduction to negotiable instruments

Neighbor Problems in India and what to do about them

Managing Court Cases with Mental Strength

Delays in Court Cases in India

Introduction to Patents and Patent Law in India